RAIN

T0284728

'*Rain* is a fascinating exploration, a celebration and a meditation on that curiously English obsession. This is an unashamedly English book, yet one far away from the problematic associations of nationalism and closer to a more deeply felt and older connection with the landscape, and that is an achievement to be celebrated in itself. Harrison is a welcome and modest companion, one who shares her extraordinary knowledge.' Katharine Norbury, *Observer*

'A nature lover's glimpse into hedgerow and lane, hilltop and woodland, blending meteorological-minded poetry, entomology and old folk idioms and pin-sharp observations about everything from berries to bird song.' *National Geographic Traveller*

'The real merit of the book is how deftly Harrison avoids the registers of piety and sentimentality in which the countryside is so often expressed. Her insights are always modest, sometimes hesitant. The world, as she sees it, telescopes into cobalt-coloured bluebells but it also opens up pathways into a more expansive sensibility.' Shahidha Bari, *FT*

RAIN

Four Walks in
English Weather

MELISSA

HARRISON

FABER & FABER

First published in 2016
by Faber & Faber Limited
Bloomsbury House
74–77 Great Russell Street
London WC1B 3DA
This paperback first published in 2017

Typeset by Faber & Faber Limited
Printed and bound by CPI Group (UK) Ltd, Croydon, CR0 4YY

A CIP record for this book
is available from the British Library

ISBN 978-0-571-32894-9

10

For Dad,
and for Mum

and
for Margaret and Tony

CONTENTS

And who art thou? said I to the soft-falling shower,
Which, strange to tell, gave me an answer,
  as here translated:
I am the poem of earth . . .
  WALT WHITMAN, *The Voice of the Rain*

The past hovering as it revisits the light.
  EDWARD THOMAS, *It Rains*

INTRODUCTION

What does rain mean to you? Do you see it as a dreaded inconvenience, a strange national obsession, or an agricultural necessity? We love to grumble about it, yet we invent dozens of terms to describe it and swap them gleefully; it trickles through our literature from Geoffrey Chaucer to Alice Oswald, and there are websites and apps that mimic its sound, soothing us while we work or sleep. Rain is what makes the English countryside so green and pleasant; it's also what swells rivers, floods farms and villages and drives people out of their homes.

Because it's something that sends most of us scurrying indoors, few people witness what actually happens out in the landscape on a wet afternoon. And yet our topography creates such unstable conditions that almost every day, as natural and inevitable as breathing, weather fronts form, clouds gather and rain falls, changing how the English countryside looks, smells and sounds, and the way the living things in it behave. And the falling rain alters the landscape itself, dissolving ancient rocks, deepening river channels and moving soil from place to place. Rain is co-author of our living countryside; it is also a part of our deep internal landscape, which is why we become fretful and uneasy when it's too long withheld. Fear it as we might, complain about it as we may, rain is as essential to our sense of identity as it is to our soil.

And there's something else that rain gives us; something deeper and more mysterious, to do with memory, and nostalgia, and a pleasurable kind of melancholy. Perhaps there have simply been too many novels with storm-drenched emotional climaxes, and too many films in which sad protagonists look out through rain-streaked windows, but it seems to me that rain is a mirror of one of our key emotional states: not a negative one at all, but deeply necessary – just as necessary as joy. Water, after all, both reflects us, and brings life; it was also, for Jung, an archetype of the unconscious, and of change. 'Into each life some rain must fall,' wrote Henry Wadsworth Longfellow (or was it Dennis Potter?) – and it's quite true: after all, nothing new can grow without it.

The idea for this book came to me in the Lake District, where I was spending a week with my husband and his parents. Cumbria has some of the highest levels of rainfall in the entire UK, and when we go there we go prepared: 'There's no such thing as bad weather, only unsuitable clothing,' as the redoubtable Alfred Wainwright said. That day, we walked from Keswick to Threlkeld along an old railway track in full waterproof gear (even the dog had her coat on) and it absolutely *hossed* it down, as the locals say. But – unlike in December 2015, when much heavier rain and flooding devastated the area – it was wonderful: we were dry and warm inside our clothes, the River Greta rushed and roared white, a dipper dinked smartly from the gleaming rocks and the leaves dripped green and glossy on the trees. We saw a couple of other walkers out with their dogs, but really there was hardly anyone about. It seemed such a waste.

To write a book about rain I had to get used to going outside and getting wet, as we did that day. I visited four parts of the countryside in showery weather and, when others looked apprehensively at the sky and went indoors, I put on waterproofs and headed out – in some cases, several times. I have blended these expeditions with reading, research, memory and a little conjecture in order to describe, I hope without undue distortion, the course of four rain-showers as they pass over English soil.

This book does not pretend to be an exhaustive survey of the country's natural history during precipitation, and nor is it a purely scientific investigation into a meteorological phenomenon; instead, it's an imaginative account of how England – human, animal and vegetable – weathers, and is weathered by, the storm.

MELISSA HARRISON, January 2016

I

WICKEN FEN

January

Kelching: raining hard

Midnight rains
Make drowned fens.

LINCOLNSHIRE PROVERB

It is the end of January 2014, and I feel as though it has been raining for weeks. Large parts of the South London park where we walk our dog are under water, and it barely seems worth towelling the mud from her fur between one walk and the next. With a blocked gutter and an extremely dilatory landlady we lie awake and listen to water spilling down our bedroom window night after night; eventually, part of the exterior wall becomes saturated and I have to move all my clothes out of the cupboard as mildew begins to take hold.

It's far worse elsewhere. The Somerset Levels have flooded, drained, and flooded again, the Eastern fen country is full of water, and right across the country rivers roil high and brown, burst their banks or are in spate. Farmers lose crops and see their grassland die; friends are washed out of their homes; tragically, people drown. The rain continues regardless, with the stubborn, set-in quality of a child who cries without expectation of help.

In December 2013 parts of the country had double their usual amount of precipitation, and the TV tells us we're having the wettest January for 250 years. Blame America, say the weathermen; their severe winter weather (or 'polar vortex', as the media has dubbed it) created too much of a contrast between its bitter, freezing air and the warmer climate to the south. That's strengthened the jet stream and, in turn, the stormy depressions that run east along it towards Britain – and the mild, Atlantic air it's brought tends to hold more water. The larger truth is, it's unlikely to be a one-off; we may all need to get used to more extreme weather conditions, more often, as the long hangover from the excesses of our industrial revolution begins to bite.

I decide to visit the place where Britain first learned how to live in partnership with water – because, like many hard-won lessons, it's something we may be in danger of forgetting. The Fens were in large part drained, but have never quite been conquered; today, in fact, we are restoring some areas converted to agriculture to their original role, and returning other parts to the sea.

The Fens are a low-lying area consisting mainly of peat (vegetable matter laid down by decaying plants) and silt (fine mineral matter deposited by water) around the Wash, on the border of Norfolk and Lincolnshire. Once a vast, waterlogged marsh, now only 0.1 per cent of the original Great Fen Basin remains as true wild fen, in four tiny fragments: Wicken Fen, Holme Fen, Woodwalton and Chippenham. The rest, for the most part, is farmed.

Into the fen country four major rivers and a number of tributaries drain rainfall collected from four million acres of higher ground in several counties. The rain that collects there has been managed for centuries in different ways, from Roman dykes to modern pumping stations, and from Dutchman Cornelius Vermuyden's seventeenth-century drainage work to the Victorians' system of windmills and today's electric pumps. Yet 1,500 years of such ingenuity is more than matched by the tough Fenlanders themselves, who once used everything from boats to stilts and jumping poles to traverse the waterlogged landscape, and made their living, before the fen country was drained and farmed, from wildfowling, fishing, and turf- and sedge-cutting. Now one of the country's most fertile and productive agricultural areas, containing about half of the top-quality growing soil in the whole of England, the spirit of the original 'fen tigers' lives on in the fierce independence and no-nonsense practicality of the Lincolnshire, Cambridgeshire, Suffolk and Norfolk natives who still populate this watery place. Here, the fens' power, and their value, has long been clearly understood – not only in modern terms of biodiversity conservation or regional hydromorphology, but with a deeper respect: a sense, now proving true, that this marshy landscape exists here for a reason.

Oddly enough the flat, wet area between Cambridge

and the Wash is one of the driest in Britain in terms of rainfall, partly because it gets little or no orographic precipitation, or rainfall sparked by clouds drifting over high ground – one of the reasons mountainous areas such as Wales, Cumbria and Dartmoor experience such a lot of wet weather. But on a mild, dull day in late January what blankets both my home, in South London, and my destination, the area just north-east of Cambridge, is stratiform precipitation falling from nimbostratus: rain caused by warm air rising gently and slowly over a cold front and condensing into water droplets. It's that grey, unchanging kind of wet weather that can spread over vast areas and doesn't go anywhere fast.

Driving towards East Anglia the sky gradually gets bigger; even on a day like today, grey and dim, it becomes enormous, taking up a good three quarters of the view. Eventually we find ourselves in flat, arable land with rich black earth and roads as straight as rulers: fen country. I gaze out through the car's passenger window on which droplets of water shiver and break backwards; beyond the glass the wet fields unfurl to the unforgiving line of the horizon. In the boot the dog is hunkered down and probably car-sick, enduring the journey for the sake of the dream-rabbits at its end.

Slowly the GPS homes us in on our destination: the little village of Wicken and the National Trust's oldest nature reserve, Wicken Fen. Incredibly species-rich, like ancient woodland or true wild-flower meadows, this fragment of wild fen is also an excellent place to see how man and nature together can work with, rather than against, water.

The villages in this part of the country – the cities too, like Ely with its heart-stopping cathedral – are usually built on 'fen islands': firmer areas of greensand or boulder clay which support their foundations better than the treacherous peat. In one village a bungalow boasts a front garden full of dripping gnomes and knick-knacks; next door its neighbour's leafless apple tree has dropped its yellow fruit all over the sodden lawn. Everywhere, collared doves crouch on the telephone wires, puffed up against the damp.

In Wicken village the verges are starred with early primroses, and one we pass is stalked by two green woodpeckers sporting red military caps. Still known in many parts of the country as yaffles, they are looking for ants, using their beaks to disturb underground chambers and extracting them with their long, sticky tongues. In autumn, wood ants retreat to their thermo-regulated anthills, but common ants move to chambers deep below the frost line and enter 'diapause', a state of semi-hibernation, until spring; these, fooled by the mild temperatures brought by the Gulf Stream, must have woken early. Ants are well attuned to the weather: many people believe even now that their movements predict rain, and certainly the little mounds of earth they construct around their burrow entrances do an excellent job of stopping rainwater running into them.

'You're keen,' says the man in the Trust's information centre, cocking an eye at the weather: apart from a couple of diehard birders with their gaiters and monopods it looks as though we'll have the place to ourselves. Today, he tells us, the fen is full of water, so much of the reserve is a no-go area. The dog quivers with expectation as we talk, keen to get on with the walk now that we're here: not for her the information boards or gift shop. As for the rain, she couldn't care less.

The fact that large parts of Wicken Fen are waterlogged is just as it should be, the peat, sedge and reed beds holding on to today's rainfall rather then letting it pour away to cause flooding elsewhere. But we can walk along the raised banks of Wicken Lode, which was dug in Roman times to drain this part of the fen and take water from it into the River Cam and thence to the Great Ouse and out to sea, and was used to transport peat and sedge until about 1940. It's shallow, navigable only by small boats; much of it is now permitted to be used only by the local Fenlanders, in recognition of their ancient right. It passes as slow and silver as mercury between stands of pale golden *Phragmites* reed shot through here and there with blood-red bramble stolons. The rain falling all around us is almost silent as it dimples the surface of the lode, but the reeds' feathery pennants whisper and susurrate to themselves as we pass. Deeper and more distant than the reeds' speech, though, is the rushing-water sound of a breeze we can't yet feel as it hits the faraway alder and buckthorn carrs. The dog trots ahead of us, alert and keyed up: while heavy rain can wash scent from the ground, moisture makes some airborne smells more volatile, so the world she moves through today may well be denser with information.

The earth of the levee on which we walk is pitch-dark peat marbled with paler Gault clay and silt slubbed out from the lode each year. Twin desire paths, made by pairs of people walking, are worn through the dull winter grass like parallel wheel ruts; here and there they merge in a mire of sticky, 'loving' mud that cakes our boots and leaves an ashen cast on the trodden-down grass beyond. Here and there are little black mounds; one has a freshwater mussel shell in it, dug out from somewhere deep on the bank, while others are fibrous with fragments of *Phragmites* root. While severe flooding and intense cold sends moles deep underground, wet weather can result in an increase in molehills. Shallow, damp, less compacted soil is easier for them to work, and this reduction in energy expenditure, along with abundant food sources, leads to better health and lower

[9]

mortality – and increased breeding compared to that in prolonged dry spells.

Rain on soil also brings moles' food source, worms, to the surface, as every bait fisherman, foot-stamping gull and worm-charming child knows. It used to be thought that they were trying to escape drowning, but new studies have suggested this may not be the case; it takes far more than a few showers to render soil uninhabitable for most invertebrates. As with moles, damp surface soil is easier for worms to move through – and it may be that they are taking the opportunity, when it rains, to strike out for new and less crowded ground. Some species, like the floodplain earthworm (*Octolasion tyrtaeum*), cope particularly well in waterlogged soil, and parts of the country that flood regularly tend to contain greater numbers of these types of invertebrate. Areas unused to regular flooding are usually home to more such creatures per square metre of soil, but are left with far fewer after a serious flood because the species are not adapted to inundation. It can take many years to build invertebrate numbers back up again after a big loss, with knock-on effects on the fertility and drainage of the soil.

To the left of the levee banks of brambles form massy humps, crabbed and tangled as though concealing something troubling within. There are a few bare hawthorns hung with silver drops, while on the other side of the lode young silver birches have been recently cleared and the trunks piled up to decay naturally; longhorn cattle and rare konik ponies brought in by the National Trust help keep down the rest of the scrub that is threatening to make woodland of the precious grazing marsh. Here and there hazels have produced their yellow catkins; there are hips bright as blood, too, and beside the path a straggle of field mustard, most likely a farmland escapee, blooms yellow and incongruous against the grey January sky: I crush a little between my fingers for its peppery smell and wonder whether spring may not be so far away after all.

Wet days like today seemed interminable when I was a child. Being stuck indoors was the most terrible punishment: outside was where everything exciting happened. Apart from *Blue Peter*, *Jackanory* and *Noel Edmonds' Multi-coloured Swap Shop* there was rarely anything good on TV, and although I remember my Dad bringing home a Sinclair ZX81 when I was six, it was only my brother who, following after hours of laborious programming, could cause it to display primitive and largely inexplicable games on our old, wood-panelled TV. The best thing about our house – big enough for six children, full of books, but hopelessly shabby – was the garden with its three ancient cooking-apple trees that were excellent for climbing; a monolithic, impregnable weeping willow, home to woodpeckers, treecreepers and nuthatches; a frog-busy pond made from an old bath;

tangly areas excellent for making camps, and an old air-raid shelter at the far end upon whose sloping roof, in summer, my four elder sisters sometimes sunbathed. It was this little kingdom that wet weather denied us.

And there was more. On fine days we had the run of the local woods (now a paintballing centre and fenced off); we rode our bikes or rollerskated around the village, and the next village a couple of miles away; we explored the fields between the house and our primary school and only went home when we were hungry. A really wet day – Mum, at her typewriter, would shoo us outdoors if it was just a little drizzly – meant the reduction of that vast territory to the smaller, duller enclave of the house itself, and we chafed at it. Yet that circumscribed world is now all that's available to many modern kids: studies suggest that since the 1970s, when I was born, children's 'radius of activity' – the area around their home in which they are allowed to play unsupervised – has declined by almost 90 per cent. Perhaps every day – not just when it rains – is an indoor day for children now.

A watery sun breaks briefly through the cloud and dazzles off the lode as a kingfisher unzips the air above the water. A blue dart, understood only in the inarticulate half-second after it passes, it almost takes the heart from my chest. Briefly, the day feels illuminated – but just a few steps on we find a dead shrew on the path, sodden but unmarked; they're not good swimmers, and with water levels high and large parts of the fen currently underwater it's likely it was washed out of its burrow and drowned. This can happen with water voles too, who become an easy meal, if forced onto dry land, for mink and birds of prey.

A heron flaps effortfully over our heads, making for the mere where crowds of wigeon drift and whistle. 'Nice weather for ducks,' we say, ruefully — and with some reason: waterbirds' feathers have an oily coating, renewed by preening, that makes them waterproof and helps them trap air to keep them warm and buoyant. Weather like this really is water off a duck's back: a recent study found that farm ducks actively enjoyed a light shower, although many waterfowl will take shelter from particularly heavy rain simply to conserve heat and energy.

After twenty minutes or so we strike away from the lode into flat farmland. Some of the fields have recently been ploughed and it's good to see the rich, dark furrows; some are baized with young crops, but others have been left as stubble over winter, a return to pre-war practices that benefits birds, insects and wild flowers enormously. At the faraway field margins the hedges appear khaki: the long, wet winter has encouraged algae to colonise the bark. Closer at hand I find a single, tiny

speedwell in flower, its blueness cowered in to itself;
like the daisy, its petals close in wet weather to pre-
vent its pollen being washed away. The coal-coloured
field beyond looks as though it's been recently drilled,
perhaps for winter wheat or barley. Until it comes up
there's no way to know.

Arable country is much less decipherable to out-
siders than it once was. Modern cropping has become
more varied, more scientific and perhaps more opaque,
and we laymen have largely lost interest in where our
food comes from beyond what's written reassuringly
on the packet; there's a disconnect now that my lovely
old Ladybird books, with their watercolour illustrations
of tractors and gulls and talk of sowing and ploughing
and harvest time, didn't seem to assume. Once they've
properly broken ground I can recognise wheat, barley,
oats and maize, and everyone can do rapeseed these
days when it's in flower, but I can't identify many of
the vegetables or legumes as they grow, or distinguish
the cover crops; I'm not sure whether those are scat-
tered swedes or sugar beets in a field we pass, and I
don't know why they haven't been gathered up. I see
the tractors out on the land, and it gives me a warm feeling, something primordial and bucolic to do with things
being as they should be – but for the most part I can't
guess what they're doing. It is a loss.

Here and there the huge, dried umbellifers of hogweed are silhouetted against a sky smudged white and lemon at the horizon, which seems very far away. The muddy farm track we walk is pitted with the tiny, precise slots of muntjac deer, and where water stands in the tractor ruts it reflects the dull January skies in lozenges of rain-dimpled steel. Deep in the hedge, among the new spears of arum breaking ground, are some fly-tipped engine-oil bottles, newspapers and sodden carpet, while moss is turning the damp edges of the shadier rides emerald-green.

A grid of narrow dykes here collects rain from the fields and feeds it into the watercourses, and because of the weather, levels are high and are likely to remain so through spring. In a month or two the dykes will be full of frogspawn and, when the warm weather comes, grass snakes, but for now they're home to fish, from pike to roach to little sticklebacks, fierce-fanged dragonfly larvae that will decimate the tadpoles when they hatch, sluggish frogs hibernating in the mud and leaf litter at the bottom, and – far fewer these days, but there nonetheless – overwintering eels as long as a man's arm.

As we walk, the muffled thud of guns reaches our ears over the constant patter of rain on our waterproof hoods: someone indifferent to the weather is out shooting pigeons, which feed in flocks at this time of year and make for easy targets. The guns aren't the only ones after them, either; a pile of wet feathers, still bloody at the root, betrays a sparrowhawk's plucking post somewhere in the branches above us. The hawk herself – a female; the males, or 'muskets', aren't large enough to take a pigeon – is hunched in a leafless ash tree two fields away. Well fed, she can wait out the weather, merely shaking the silver beads every so often from her smooth, grey back and barred breast – though if it lasts too long she will be forced to hunt regardless. I tramp on through the mud, compulsively reciting to myself the opening lines of Alison Brackenbury's lovely poem, 'Brockhampton':

The land was too wet for ploughing; yet it is done.
Even the stones of the ridges lie sulky and brown.
The roads are a slide of mud. The wet sky
Is blank as the chink of the hawk's perfect eye . . .
  from 'Brockhampton', 1995

As the sun sinks lower, and the temperature falls, the pattering rain slows imperceptibly and stops – and within moments we are rioted around by goldfinches with their end-of-school chatter; there are sudden greenfinches in the hedges, too, and great tits calling, and the silvery notes of a robin trickle like water from somewhere in the carr. They've been waiting out the rain and now's their last chance to feed before darkness falls, so they must make the most of it: it is as though the landscape has shaken birds from its hedges and thickets as my dog shakes water from her fur.

The air is soft and clear but the day's rain continues to sink silently into the fields and fens. The land here is so flat it will hold on to the water for a long time before it drains north-east towards the Wash; but drain it will: first into the peat, then by degrees into the field drains and lodes, and to the tributaries, passing through pumping stations and locks and sluices as it goes, then into the River Witham, the Welland, the Nene or the Great Ouse, and eventually into the chill North Sea. As it flows, the dykes and watercourses will be lined with another layer of fine silt; the course of old, lost rivers can still be seen across arable land in the Fens, raised up, counter-intuitively, above the surrounding land by layers of sediment, and known as roddons.

The peat here began forming 4,500 years ago, and as long as it's kept wet it can lock up thirty times more carbon than if the same area was forested: a precious natural resource. Once it was cut and dried for fuel, and nowadays its rain-retentive properties have led it to be prized by gardeners – though awareness is growing of the devastating effects of peat extraction, in terms of habitat loss, carbon release and flood defence. Over-drainage, to create farmland, also damages peat bogs and fens; unlike a bathroom sponge, when peat has dried out it shrinks and never swells again, which is why large parts of the Fens now lie well below sea level. At Holme Fen an iron post was sunk right down into the peat in the middle years of the nineteenth century; its top now stands four metres above ground level.

During that time the ability of these areas to absorb water, and defend us against floods, has been greatly reduced, so that when meltwater and heavy rains combine to overwhelm the Fenland rivers – as happened, devastatingly, in 1947 – or the sea walls necessary to protect the drained land are breached – as in 1953, with the loss of 307 lives – there's precious little left to contain the floods. That's why these days, low-lying East Anglia needs artificial drainage and vast coastal defences to keep it from being overwhelmed – yet even so, in December 2013 thousands of homes across three counties here had to be evacuated as huge surges demolished sea walls. Seaside towns were flooded, seven cliff-top homes collapsed, farms, wildlife and businesses were destroyed, and two people lost their lives. Afterwards, Norman Lamb, the MP for North Norfolk, described the area as 'like a war zone'. But here's the thing about water: the more it is denied the more powerful its incursions become. No wonder many people now believe that with sea levels rising, the Fens, with their protective, buffering function developed over thousands of years, should be restored, and swathes of agricultural land – some of it reclaimed from the sea as recently as the 1970s – finally relinquished.

We turn back towards the village. Around us crows and jackdaws are beginning to assemble for the night; they wheel and parry over a stubble field near the mere, calling, calling, while a hundred garrulous starlings gather in an ash. Soon they'll seek more flocks until they join up in a vast murmuration and sweep down on the reed beds to roost. I'm glad of my binoculars then, as we see, across the mere, a tall, stag-headed oak decorated with what I suddenly realise are cormorants: heraldic, prehistoric, facing in every direction as though gathering in the last of the light.

In a sudden, late dazzle of low evening sun our three shadows track us on the reeds across the lode, and a single, heavy bullrush nods to us as though in investiture as we pass it by for the second time. The light is low and clear and turns the reed beds red; it lingers longest on the topmost feathers, gilding them rich copper, but the still, undimpled water they are rooted in is turning deep blue now, not silver, reflecting the darkening sky above.

In the village pub everyone knows each other: teenage girls in short skirts, sixty-something farmers, local tradespeople, village wives and old Fenlanders alike. Warm and convivial, loud with gossip underflowed by the tintinnabulation of the slots, it offers chips, chips, chips with everything. And crocodile steaks.

But around the pub the village sprawls silent and almost pitch-dark, apart from a lit red phone box with no telephone in it. In the darkness, the rain – which this winter seems never to stop for very long – begins to patter invisibly once more on its blistered roof and streak its ancient, cloudy panes.

2

SHROPSHIRE

April

Blunks: sudden showers

A sunshiny shower
Never lasts half an hour.

ENGLISH PROVERB

Shropshire: a rural landscape of woods and fields, market towns, canals and once-busy Victorian industrial sites now sinking back into quiet obscurity. It's just after lunch on Easter Sunday, and across the nation people, including me, are planning to go for a walk. Of course, the farmers and dog-walkers and hardy hiking types are out all year round; but today they'll be joined by the twice-a-year strollers, the dutiful family visitors and the buggies-and-toddlers brigade. Everyone hopes for a little sunshine on Easter weekend; it's a chance to stretch our legs after winter and see a bit of the countryside. The weather, however, doesn't always agree: over the long Easter weekend in 1998, for instance, a band of heavy rain sat unmoving over the whole of Shropshire, causing floods which resulted in five deaths.

But not this year. The Chelmarsh and Lake Vyrnwy reservoirs may be full, and everywhere groundwater levels are high; we're not expecting a hosepipe ban this year. But at last the long, wet winter seems to be behind us. The showers that are blowing in and over today are of a very different character to January's set-in rain.

In Joseph Taylor's 1812 book, *The Complete Weather Guide*, he says of April:

> The distinguishing characteristic of the weather during this month is fickleness; the most lovely sunshiny days are succeeded by others, which by the force of contrast often seem the most unpleasant of any in the year . . . the vicissitudes of warm gleams and gentle showers have a most powerful effect in hastening that universal springing of the vegetable tribes, whence the season derives its appellation.
>
> JOSEPH TAYLOR, *The Complete Weather Guide: A Collection of Practical Observations for Prognosticating the Weather, Drawn from Plants, Animals, Inanimate Bodies, and Also by Means of Philosophical Instruments,* 1812

Sunshine and rain and everything growing: that sounds about right. No wonder Chaucer opened *The Canterbury Tales* with April showers.

I've been coming to Shropshire for ten years now to visit my husband's parents, who live in a little village near the Wrekin, a large, dramatic hill not far from the M54. At first the area was slow to reveal its beauty; having grown up in love with Dartmoor, where my grandparents lived and where we spent two weeks every summer, I immediately loved the upland landscape of

Carding Mill Valley ('little Switzerland', the locals call it – not unreasonably, either) and Wenlock Edge's craggy outcrops, but the unpretentious farmland that makes up the bulk of the county seemed at first to have neither the cosy charm of the West Country nor the wide-open appeal of the Fens. It crept up on me, though: a worked, and working, landscape, full of cows and sheep and largely unbothered by tourists. As for conurbations, there's Shrewsbury, of course, and Telford, but the county has no cities at all; in fact, Shropshire is a challenge for many people to find on a map. But now I have its measure, like music heard enough times to become intelligible. When I walk its narrow lanes, as I will today, the landscape around me, its hedges and fields and farms, has a particularity – half seen, half sensed – that I can't help but respond to.

I leave the dog drowsing by the woodburner; she's been out once already today, and without her it's easier to tune into the *haeccitas*, the 'thisness' of the place, without worrying that she's about to belt off in pursuit of something furry. Half-terrier, born a farm dog in Ireland, she lived as a stray for her first eighteen months and the hunting instinct dies hard.

Pulling the front door to I pause for a moment, looking out at the wet driveway where a wren shouts a spring trill from the hedge. My parents-in-law are selling their house and moving to the South-East, and this is the last time I'll be in the village. It may not be my home, but it's somewhere I've taken shelter, and I know I'm going to miss coming here.

I could walk up the Wrekin, but on Easter Sunday it's likely to be busy – and having come up from London for the weekend it's nice to leave the crowds behind. I decide to take a meandering route around the village that will lead me through the lanes, across a couple of fields and back. It rained not half an hour ago and water beads the roofs and bonnets of the cars in the drive, but above me massy cumulus pursue one another across blue April skies, stately and white.

Britain's prevailing wind comes from the south-west, but today it blows from the north-west and brings a little Polar chill on its breath. While over the cold sea it hardly thawed, but in the spring sunshine the good, rich earth of Wales, along with the rest of the British Isles, has been warming up, heating the air above it and causing it to rise and condense like breath, and the water it bears to form droplets heavy enough to fall as rain. Now, shower clouds are processing inland to the Welsh Marches, the West Midlands and beyond, shedding rain as they go. They will dissipate slowly as darkness falls and the temperature drops again, and the night will be dry – but until then it's sunshine and showers; barely have the tiles dried on the village roofs than another blows in. 'April showers,' we say to one another, casting a judicious eye at the heavens – although statistically, April is a relatively dry month across most of Britain. But it is changeable; rainclouds tend to build and blow in (and over) quickly, and it's not always easy to tell, at the start of each day, whether the weather will hold.

April is all about change on the ground, too. Deep in the warm, damp earth seeds are germinating, the hedgerows are coming into leaf, wild flowers are beginning to bloom and insects breed, and everywhere the birds are at their most active, building nests and defending their territories. Life is getting on with the grand business of growing and reproducing; rain may feel like an inconvenience, but at this time of year it's essential.

Near the church I see that the two horse chestnuts, which came into leaf first out of all the big trees in the village, are now starting to produce their flower-spikes: huge, creamy candles that will blaze into life in a couple of weeks and release pollen, marking the start of the hay-fever season. Showery weather will help wash it from the atmosphere; today, though, the pollen is still locked up safely inside the ripening green buds.

The horse chestnuts' leaves are already marked with the brown scribbles made by leaf miner larvae, which live between the upper and lower cuticles in a tunnel safe from the elements. Despite this, the clever blue tits here and in several other places across the British Isles have worked out how to get at them, and their acrobatic abilities and low body weight make it easy for them to hang from the floppy leaves to feed. And now that the blue tits' eggs have started to hatch, these towering conker trees are seeing a surge in visitors, keen to feed their hungry young.

The leaf miners are just one part of a huge caterpillar explosion that takes place across the country at about this time of year, and around which many birds' nesting seasons must fit: soft, moist caterpillars are the perfect baby food for fledglings, so mating needs to be carefully timed. But spring is coming earlier to our latitude these days, and while some birds are changing their behaviour to keep up – swallows now arrive about a week earlier than in 1970 – others have been slower to react, and it's thought that as time goes on those birds that rely on single food sources may prove unable to adapt.

These leaf miners may be protected from the rain in their tunnels, but it's sluicing some of the bigger caterpillars, like those of the sawfly and purple hairstreak, from the oak trees by the lane; they drop into the churchyard where opportunistic ground-feeding blackbirds and robins will tidy them up once the shower has passed. For now, only the mistle thrush, or stormcock, is out in the wet: he's earning his country name by perching on the top of the church porch and singing lustily. Even from the lane I can see his throat working and his speckled breast feathers puffed out against the rain.

It's felt like spring for a good month now, but only now are some of the other big trees catching up with the horse chestnuts. The old saw goes:

> *If the oak's before the ash*
> *Then you'll get only a splash.*
> *If the ash is before the oak*
> *Then you may expect a soak.*

In the little spinney on the edge of the village the ash leaves are still wrapped in sticky black buds, but everywhere the oaks are bursting into leaf: a dry summer ahead, then. Soft and copper-coloured for a little while, maturing quickly to green and then darkening and toughening by August, their topmost leaves are usually the first to unfurl – and will be the first to be lost later in the year.

Those topmost leaves are where the shower hits first: the faintest rain-patter, a few flung drops on the breeze that sparkle here and there on those glossy copper cuticles and speckle my waterproof coat. Then a grey, laden shower cloud obscures the sun, and I put up my hood.

Beyond the last houses the road breaks between pastures in which the rain is helping the grass grow, boosting its 'D-value', or digestibility. The early grass, before it starts producing seed-heads, is the most nutritious for sheep and cows, and makes the best fodder for later in the year, too. The dairy farmers want good growing conditions early on so they can get their herds out from under cover where feed costs them money; the sheep farmers, too, want to get the new lambs out on grass – and good D-values require plenty of sunshine, and just enough rain. In 1957 this entire region remained utterly rainless throughout April; May had a little, but the grass never quite caught up and extra fodder for livestock had to be bought in. The arable farmers did no better: with poor growing conditions in springtime yields were way down come harvest. A dry spring can have consequences that echo through the entire growing season, affecting the prices we pay for our fruit and vegetables – and meat and dairy – in the shops.

One reason we know how much rain has fallen where, and when, is the British Rainfall Organisation: a quintessentially eccentric body and one of the first examples of what we now call 'citizen science'. George James Symons, who began his working life in the Meteorological Department at the Board of Trade, set up the Association in the middle of the nineteenth century in response to public concern that rainfall was decreasing across the British Isles. He recruited a small network of initial observers, then wrote to *The Times* in 1863 listing the further locations he wanted, calling for observers 'of both sexes and all ages' and offering to subsidise the costs of instruments. By 1867 he had 1,300 observers and had to leave his post at the Board of Trade; by his death in 1900 there were 3,408, drawn from 'nearly every social grade from peer to peasant'. Symons ran the Organisation on strictly egalitarian principles, emphasising cooperation at all times and ensuring that decisions were made collectively. But ensuring his observers felt valued was more than just tact or idealism on Symons' part; after all, it was their subscriptions that paid almost the entire running costs of the project.

Symons was eventually made a Fellow of the Royal Society and a Chevalier of the *Ordre national de la Légion d'honneur*. Thirty or so years after his death one young Rotherham recorder, Vernon Radcliffe, visited the London house he once lived in to see his famous rain gauge. When he reported its poor condition to Dr John Glasspoole, President of the Royal Meteorological Society, word of his impertinence got back to Radcliffe's headmaster – and Radcliffe was told in no uncertain terms to stop meddling. It seems the schoolboy defied his teacher, though, for not only did he go on to become resident observer at the King's Observatory, Kew, he was awarded an MBE in 1997 for his work as a voluntary rainfall observer, one of thousands whose painstakingly amassed data provided then, and still provides, an invaluable climatological record.

In 1916 the BRO was called upon to determine whether the use of artillery on the Western Front was somehow responsible for one of the wettest winters on record, something that, in the mud of the trenches, must have seemed horribly possible. But upon consulting their meteorological records the opinion given by its then director, Dr Hugh Robert Mill, was that there was no connection between gunfire and precipitation. The following winter would prove less wet, despite the artillery barrage of the Somme, but bitterly cold.

The BRO was finally transferred to the Met Office after the War, in 1919, but continued to publish its records until 1991; they are still used today.

Joseph Taylor's *Weather Guide* says:

> Early in [April], that welcome guest and harbinger
> of summer, the swallow, returns . . . at first, here and
> there, only one appears, glancing by as if scarcely
> able to endure the cold. But in a few days their num-
> ber is greatly increased, and they sport with much
> seeming pleasure in the warm sunshine . . .

I'm hoping to spot some swallows while I'm out, but today they are nowhere to be seen. It may be that the local birds have not yet returned from Africa and Asia – or they may have arrived, seen the showery weather and nipped back to the warmer Continent for a few days. Swallows don't put on weight before their migration, as some other birds do, so they must feed as they go – and on arrival, they'll need to find something to eat pretty fast. Studies have shown that aerial plankton, the tiny flies and spiders that float on air currents and which birds like swifts and swallows eat, are pushed along before a weather front, quickly 'scrubbed' from the air by precipitation and then begin to ascend again as soon as thermals return after a shower – which might explain the old saw:

> *Low flies the swallow,*
> *Rain to follow;*
> *But when swallows fly high*
> *The weather will be dry.*

The village is far behind me now, its squat church tower lost in trees. The lane I walk is flanked by hawthorn hedges, and on the verges glossy hart's tongue ferns funnel the rain so it puddles in their centres where the new fronds unfurl. There are bluebells, too; not the pushy, varicoloured hybrids that colonise my London garden, but English bluebells hung with silver drops, delicately drooped like a shepherd's crook, and with a curious luminosity to their cobalt flowers. A woodland plant, their flowering period is timed to take advantage of the gap between the soil warming up and the canopy closing as trees come into leaf; in a dry spell their bulbs have the ability to pull themselves, by means of special contracting roots, further down into the ground, where rainfall like today's keeps the soil moister.

There's stitchwort, too, and occasional dandelions like big brass buttons in the hedge-bank, and here and there the cow parsley is just starting to come out. I remember Edward Thomas's poem 'It Rains', with its lovely sense of the lushness of spring rain on new green growth, and its clear sense of rain's oblique relationship to memory and the past:

> It rains, and nothing stirs within the fence
> Anywhere through the orchard's untrodden, dense
> Forest of parsley. The great diamonds
> Of rain on the grassblades there is none to break,
> Or the fallen petals further down to shake.
>
> And I am nearly as happy as possible
> To search the wilderness in vain though well,
> To think of two walking, kissing there,
> Drenched, yet forgetting the kisses of the rain:
> Sad, too, to think that never, never again,
>
> Unless alone, so happy shall I walk
> In the rain. When I turn away, on its fine stalk
> Twilight has fined to naught, the parsley flower
> Figures, suspended still and ghostly white,
> The past hovering as it revisits the light.

EDWARD THOMAS, 'It Rains', 1917

I've only seen one other person on my walk so far, a man walking two miniature dachshunds in little waterproof coats, and I wonder how busy it is up on the Wrekin; whether, if I was a crow flying over it with crankshaft wingbeats I'd look down to see a line of bright anoraks and raincoats straggling across its long back, and hear the children calling and laughing and racing ahead.

When I was at school one of the most heady of announcements was that of 'wet break'. A large, unprepossessing comprehensive composed in no small part of damp, prefab outbuildings, it had hardly any proper outside space aside from a bleak tarmac playground and one small, muddy games pitch, so, unlike at home, staying indoors didn't seem much of a loss; instead, brief anarchy would reign in the drab classrooms and corridors as, intoxicated by the temporary licence, we ran, raised our voices, sat on the desks and generally behaved indoors as we would out. It's strange how clearly I can still recall the way the drenched, deserted playground looked through shower-streaked classroom windows, squalls blowing across it to create shifting curtains of rain.

In the woods on the slopes of the Wrekin groups of shy fallow deer will be lying up and ruminating under the cover of dense yews, waiting for dusk when they'll emerge from cover to graze. At this time of year they live in separate herds of bucks and does: the bucks will soon start to cast their antlers ready for a new set, while many of the does are now pregnant, and will break from the herd to give birth alone in May or June. When occasional raindrops plop down on them through the yews' dark branches they flick their big ears and every so often shiver their coats. Thirty miles away, in Mortimer Forest, there's a unique herd of fallows with long coats and strange ear-tufts; but the herd here is of the ordinary kind.

Deer aren't the only creatures sheltering in the woods and waiting for dusk. The tawny owls I'd hear calling if I walked this way after dark are tucked away out of the rain; they have to stay dry as their plumage doesn't hold up at all well in damp conditions. Owls' powdery feathers are designed to be totally silent in flight; they have a downy upper surface, and 'fimbriate' or serrated margins that muffle the rushing sound of air over their wings as they fly. These adaptations mean that they become waterlogged far more easily than other birds, so in all but the direst of need owls will wait out wet weather, rather than hunt. It's why they usually choose covered places to nest, like holes in trees, squirrel dreys and owl boxes: not just to protect the young chicks from rainfall, but the parents when they're incubating the eggs.

The shower cloud blows over, taking its shadow with it across the fields; the sun dazzles briefly off the wet road with its seam of compressed dung, and everything sparkles. April is a good month for leverets, and I know that hares have been seen just outside the village in recent weeks; as I walk I try to tune my eyes to spot their small, brown shapes in the fields on either side. Unlike rabbits, hares don't sleep or breed underground; instead, they create shallow scrapes or depressions called forms in which they lie up and rest with their black-tipped ears flat back. They tend to choose fairly exposed sites so they can see all around them; hares' eyes are positioned to give them nearly 360-degree vision, so they'll have plenty of warning of predators. But not taking cover does mean that when it rains they get wet. Fortunately – and unlike rabbits – they have a special layer of fur that helps to keep off the worst of the weather; they're also excellent swimmers and have been seen to cross rivers; and with no warren to tie them down and excellent topographical awareness they can simply move to drier ground if the land becomes too waterlogged.

If there are any hares around I can't see them; I just hope they're not getting too wet. I decide to take a footpath that runs along the top of a paddock and back to the village. Two comma butterflies dance low over the lush spring grass of the paddock; they spiral, rising and falling, as though describing in air the structure of their own urgent DNA. Really heavy precipitation can knock butterflies from the air, damaging their wings or leaving them at risk from opportunistic predators, so at the first sign of approaching bad weather they'll tuck themselves away, clinging to the undersides of leaves or creeping into tall grass. But when the shower passes and the sun comes out they're quick to take wing again.

On the distant slopes of the Wrekin the rain has washed the walls of the old quarries, carrying away infinitesimal amounts of minerals from the bare rock faces and minutely weakening the seams in the exposed stone. It's filled the old quarry pits by an amount too small to measure, and in the wooded areas is already being sucked up by the oaks' and ashes' thirsty roots. And across the county and beyond it's fallen on the backs of nesting birds, sitting tight and determined on clutches of blue, or white, or brown, or speckled eggs, or flying back and forth to feed importunate upturned gapes.

A week from now, a dust storm in the Sahara will combine with air pollution to hang over the south-east of the country, eventually to be washed out of the sky by rain and deposited on our car where it's parked in our South London street. But for now it looks as though it's going to be a fine evening in Shropshire, warm and clear, and hopefully a dry Bank Holiday Monday tomorrow. It's good to walk without my hood up so I can hear the blackbirds begin their evening performances; good, too, to note the fresh-washed clarity of the air and the way it carries sounds. If I stop walking for a moment I can hear the occasional plinks of the last raindrops falling from the trees by the road.

Coleridge may have lamented its 'dull, two-fold sound' ('An Ode to the Rain'), but in an audio diary made a few months after going blind the writer and theologian John Hull described how the sound of falling rain actually brings the invisible world around him to life:

> If only there could be something equivalent to rain falling inside then the whole of a room would take on shape and dimension. I should also say that this is an experience of beauty. Instead of being isolated, cut off, preoccupied internally, you're presented with a world, you're related to a world, you are addressed by a world.
>
> Why should this experience strike one as being beautiful? Cognition is beautiful. It is beautiful to know.
>
> *from* 'Notes On Blindness', now a short film

I'm just outside the village, the sun low and lambent, when I see it flickering over the cows' backs: a swallow – unmistakeable in its *thisness*, utterly heart-lifting – then another. Five paces on and I can hear their twittering calls. They have returned from Africa to the village where they were born, where they'll scope out last year's nests in the church tower or the rectory, and raise another generation of long-distance travellers. Perhaps this year they'll build in the eaves of my parents-in-law's house, too; the house which today I will leave for the last time. The thought of their rootedness is both comforting and bitter-sweet; the sight of them tells me, as swifts told Ted Hughes, that against all odds, the globe's still working.

3

THE DARENT VALLEY

August

Haster: a thunderstorm

A wet August never brings dearth.

ENGLISH PROVERB

It's a muggy Friday morning in August and instead of going down the steps into the Underground at Brixton, to go to work, I have climbed up to the railway platform and taken a train heading east, towards Kent. It's hardly rained for the last three weeks and I want to have a look at the River Darent (or Darenth), a tributary of the Thames that is, like all our precious chalk streams, particularly affected by drought.

I love London, but it feels stale and heavy. The leaves on the plane trees, so fresh back in May, are now dark and leathery; the parched grass in the city parks, having set seed over a month ago, has become thin and yellow-thatched. But as I sit on the grimy train, passing through Penge and Beckenham and all points east, change is coming. Low pressure has been sitting to the west of the British Isles, high pressure to the east. Warm, moist air has been stable over much of the south of the country. But in the last twenty-four hours or so, hotter, drier air from Spain's plateaux has moved up and over everything like a lid.

At about the time I get off the train, the temperature hits eighteen degrees and a cumulus cloud begins forming above a valley just south of where I am, a little, sheltered suntrap lined with trees. The atmosphere above England is already warm and carrying moisture, but this pocket of air is even warmer, and as I set out on my walk a cloud begins to grow: first becoming a cumulus congestus, then eventually spreading upwards into the dry air of the upper troposphere until ice crystals begin to form at its rapidly spreading, anvil-shaped top. It begins to process slowly north towards the Darent Valley, another cloud birthing in its wake.

Thunderclouds have long been a source of consternation and myth-making – which is hardly surprising given their dramatic and occasionally violent effects. One Leonard Digges, in his *Prognostication Everlastinge of Ryghte Good Effecte* (1571) set out some of the popular lore relating to thunder, while prudently distancing himself from it just in case it proved to be nonsense:

Somme wryte (their ground I see not) that
Sondaye's thundre shoulde brynge the death of
learned men, judges and others: Mondaye's thundre,
the death of women: Tuesdaye's thundre, plenty
of graine: Wednesdaye's thundre, the deathe of
harlottes, and other blodeshede: Thursdaye's
thundre, plentie of shepe and corne: Fridaie's
thundre, the slaughter of a great man, and other

horrible murders: Saturdaye's thundre, a generall
pestilent plague and great deathe.

> DIGGES, *Prognostication Everlastinge of Ryghte Good
> Effecte*, 1571

Digges was not alone in foretelling the future through
thunder. 'Winter thunder and summer's flood, never
boded England any good,' went the old saw, while
the popular compendium *The New Book of Knowledge*,
attributed to one 'Godfridus' and frequently repub-
lished, laid out the significance of storms in every month
of the year: in January, great winds and 'plentiful corn
and cattle'; in February 'many rich men shall die in great
sickness'; in March 'debate amongst people'. August
thunder, worryingly for me today, signifies 'the same
year sorrow, wailing of many, for many shall be sick'.

For now, though, the air may be close, the sky white
rather than its recent untroubled blue, but the thun-
derhead is still some way off. I find the Darent in the
pretty village of Shoreham where it flows in a culvert
past a couple of cosy pubs and some Kentish brick-
and-tile houses; one of them, a plaque informs me,
once lived in by the visionary landscape painter Samuel Palmer, another with a UKIP poster at an upstairs
window. I lean on the wall and look down to where
water crowfoot sways and the mysterious silhouettes
of fish drift and hold in the shallows. Typically for a

chalk stream the water is astonishingly clear.

It is in part the purity of rivers like the Darent that has been their undoing. Fed from beneath the ground by a chalk aquifer, their naturally filtered waters are exceptionally clean and require less expensive purification than other rivers – making them attractive to water companies, who like to abstract their flow. Occurring mostly in the southern UK and a couple of places in France, many pass through important agricultural areas – like here in Kent – where farmers need their water to protect thirsty crops like fruit and vegetables from failure during the growing season. But chalk streams make wonderful habitats, their alkaline water supporting vast numbers of invertebrates, brown trout and other fish, and wild flowers and birds – all of which are easily threatened by low water levels, pollution and agricultural run-off. And back in the late 1980s a series of long, rainless periods, coupled with over-abstraction, meant that this chalk stream suffered the lowest recorded flow of any river in the UK. Fortunately, much work has since been done to restore the Darent and its wildlife, and while its upper reaches sometimes run low in summer as groundwater levels fall within the chalk, this section is looking healthy.

My route takes me up to Meenfield Wood on its high ridge, the M25 invisible, but not inaudible, to the east. On the hill's flank a stark chalk cross can be seen for

miles around, its hard angles inimical to the soft, roll-
ing farmland that Samuel Palmer invested with such
luminosity in his enigmatic paintings; it may be a sign
of faith, but for me the cross lacks all profundity. Nevertheless it's worth the climb: from the top of the ridge
I can look out over a vast sweep of prosperous Kent
countryside: oast houses, golf courses, stables and cops-
es in full leaf. The day is becoming humid and still, with
a slightly claustrophobic feel.

Descending the ridge along a narrow path thick with
spent cow parsley, I find the Darent again where houses
hundreds of years old boast beautiful gardens running
down to the river. Here and there thistledown swirls on
the water's surface, destined to set seed further downstream, and a southern hawker dragonfly patrols the air
above. There are little rain flies about, too; *Anthomyia
pluvialis* are said to dance before the onset of showers,
but these are simply congregating on the white flowers
of Queen Anne's lace, or wild carrot, blooming near the
bank.

Near Castle Farm the footpath skirts some widely
ridged fields of lavender bushes, recently harvested. They
must have looked spectacular in July, richly purple and
abuzz with bees from the hives at nearby Lullingstone
Castle. Something's missing, though, and it takes me a
moment to work out that it's the songbirds. There may be
swallows hunting the water meadows, and the odd crow

or wood pigeon overhead, but it's August and everything from blackbirds to blue tits is now silent and in moult.

There are young, russet-coloured Devon cows grazing the fields a little further on, and in keeping with the uncertain weather some are standing while others lie down and chew the cud. A recent American study showed that while there was no direct link between livestock lying down and the approach of rain, cattle did spend more time in repose in chilly temperatures. Yet the bovine behaviour question is really just the last survivor from a vast and once-necessary hoard of folk wisdom about the weather. Barometers could warn of impending changes in pressure, for those who had them, and before their invention observations of cloud formations and migrating birds had their uses, but in the main, people were very much in the dark – though the survival of entire communities could ride on bringing in a good harvest. As a result, folk methods of weather prognostication used to run riot, much as today a multitude of rumoured causes of (and questionable treatments for) cancer fill a gap caused by fear and lack of information. Once, dozens of days in the calendar, not just St Swithun's, could be used to foretell the weather for the coming months; or a farmer might look at which day of the week New Year's Day fell on, study the moon and the zodiac, observe the precise colour of lightning, note where each year fell in certain patterns (for instance, every seventeenth year being bad for crops),

test the weight of salt and use a thousand other methods
to predict how much rain would come, and when.

The Shepherd of Banbury's Rules (1670) was just one
among many meteorological guides which claimed to
help accurately foretell the weather, and yearly 'almanacks' (some still being published today) both collected
together, and added to, the store of folk wisdom. Joseph
Taylor's *Weather Guide* gives us this helpful advice:

> If frogs croak more than usual; if toads issue from
> their holes in the evening in great numbers . . . if
> asses shake and agitate their ears, and bray more
> frequently than usual; if hogs shake and spoil the
> stalks of corn; if bats send forth cries, and fly into
> the house; if dogs roll on the ground, and scratch up
> the earth with their fore-feet; if cows or oxen look
> towards the heavens, and turn up their nostrils as if
> catching some smell; if oxen lick their fore-feet, and
> if oxen and dogs lie on their right side; if rats and
> mice are more restless than usual; all these are signs
> which announce rain.

Not all the old folklore was off the mark, though. Not
for nothing were weather almanacks usually ascribed to
shepherds or other rustics: there was a core of sound wisdom shared by such people that had been earned by years
of minute and necessary observation. Who but a farmer

would see at a glance that his grass appeared 'rough', and know that rain would follow? For clover, common in grass pasture, does contract its trefoliate leaves upwards when the air is damp, subtly changing the texture of a field. Likewise, many wild flowers (for instance pimpernel, also known as 'countryman's weather-glass') will close their petals at the approach of rain, and dandelion clocks fold up to protect the fluffy seeds from becoming waterlogged. By reading signs like these, country people could (and still can) foretell rain better than city folk — something the old shepherd's almanacks capitalised on.

When the Kent sky — already overcast — darkens, it does so suddenly. A restless wind gets up, bullying the muggy August air so that the ripe wheat shifts uneasily, gusts pushing its golden surface this way and that like a nap. As the first fat drops of rain hit the dry earth of the footpath I make for the shelter of the river bank, hastily zipping my camera back into its case. There's a plaque there, mounted on a tree stump carved into the shape of a big brown trout: 'Officially unveiled on 12th October 2004', it says, 'to celebrate the restoration of the River Darent'. Here and there, pond skaters at its slow, shady margins are racing for the edges as raindrops begin to disrupt the meniscus on which they depend.

The downpour that follows seems to fall with more force than mere gravity could provide, and as lightning flickers – first distantly, then much closer – and thunder rends the sky, I weigh the risks of standing beneath the bankside trees against the discomfort of getting drenched. Of course, I had known ahead of time that the weather was due to break, and have brought a fold-up anorak, but without our sophisticated forecasting systems storms like this one often took our forefathers by surprise – a particular problem for farmers and sailors.

The aptly named George Merryweather displayed his storm forecaster, the 'Tempest Prognosticator', at the Great Exhibition of 1851. Looking not unlike a miniature merry-go-round, it consisted of a circle of twelve pint bottles, each containing a little rainwater and a single leech. His idea was that, on sensing electrical activity in the atmosphere, the leeches would crawl to the top of the bottles, triggering whalebone levers connected to a bell on the topmost dome; the more times the bell rang, the greater the likelihood of an approaching storm. Merryweather had big plans for his Prognosticator, believing that it could easily be connected to the telegraph network in such a way that the bell in St Paul's, London, could be rung to signal an approaching storm. But then, he also believed that arranging the bottles in a circle would allow the leeches to see one another and not become lonely. Sadly – though perhaps not surprisingly – his plans for a leech-powered storm warning system did not come to fruition.

Behind the cumulonimbus currently discharging itself over the Darent Valley, more are forming; the afternoon will see thunder and lightning over much of the south-east of England, including London, less than twenty miles away. There, the sudden cloudbursts will clean pollen and pollution from the air; traffic will slow all over the city, and cyclists and bikers will take shelter under bridges. Storm sewers will fill up and overflow into the Thames, and polluted run-off will affect the Lea, too, lowering the water purity and affecting ecosystems right the way downstream. Beneath the teeming air the wide, brown Thames will become pockmarked and dull, and up and down Oxford Street shoppers and tourists will shriek and crowd into doorways as hard rain bounces up off the pavements in a grimy spray. It's August, and few will have brought umbrellas with them; many, in sandals or flip-flops, will squelch home later, filthy-footed.

Plus ça change. Jonathan Swift described a not dissimilar scene in his long poem 'A City Shower', set over three hundred years ago:

> *Now in contiguous drops the flood comes down,*
> *Threatening with deluge this devoted town.*
> *To shops in crowds the daggled females fly,*
> *Pretend to cheapen goods, but nothing buy.*
>
> . . .

Sweepings from butchers' stalls, dung, guts, and blood,
Drowned puppies, stinking sprats, all drenched in mud,
Dead cats, and turnip tops, come tumbling down the flood.
  from 'A City Shower', 1710

There may be fewer dead dogs and turnips these days, but today's rain will still leave the capital city fresher than it was before. It will wash the particulates from the broad leaves of the London planes where they have been collecting for weeks; it will dissolve the dog shit on the pavements and inch it towards the gutters, along with dust and dry leaves, cigarette ends and fried chicken bones and dead worker wasps.

In some parts of the South-East, hail will add to the storm's fury – though fortunately, given the vineyards and the tender, ripening hops strung on their wire frames, not here in Kent. The parson/naturalist Gilbert White's delightfully precise journals record frequent thunder and hail storms in August; for instance, on 14 August 1791 he wrote:

Late this evening a storm of thunder arose in the S., which, as usual, divided into two parts, one going to the S.W. & W. & the greater portion to the S.E. and E., & so round to the N.E. From this latter division proceeded strong, & vivid lightening till late in the night. At Headleigh there was a very heavy shower,

& some hail at E. Tisted. The lightening, & hail did much damage about the kingdom.

GILBERT WHITE, *Naturalist's Journal*, 1768–93

On 14 August 1975 a violent summer storm hit Hampstead, depositing huge hailstones and three months' worth of rain amid intense thunder and lightning. The day had been stiflingly hot, the city's 'heat island' effect adding to the build-up of warm, stagnant, moisture-carrying air; the storm was triggered by an updraught caused by the high ground of Hampstead and Highgate, and having formed, it stayed there, depositing all of its rain and hail in one area as there was little wind at cloud level to move it along. One eyewitness account published in the *Journal of Meteorology* read: 'At the height of the deluge, for about twenty minutes, this entire area ... was completely covered by a heaving off-white crust of hail nearly a foot in depth'; another reported that 'hailstones were like ping-pong balls (say 18 to 20 mm), lightning was like "machine-gun fire" and the water flowed off the heath in "waterfalls".' The storm flooded all the houses on Tufnell Park Road, some to a depth of two metres.

But it's not just rain and hail that have been reported to fall from the sky during storms. In the first century AD, Pliny the Elder documented falls of frogs and fishes, and to the great fascination of schoolchildren (including myself), reports have continued to come in from around the world ever since. As recently as 16 June 1939, for example, it was said to have rained tiny frogs on the village of Trowbridge in Wiltshire. According to the *Meteorological Magazine*:

> Mr E. Ettles, superintendent of the municipal swimming pool, stated that about 4.30 p.m. he was caught in a heavy shower of rain and, while hurrying to shelter, heard behind him a sound as of the falling of lumps of mud. Turning, he was amazed to see hundreds of tiny frogs falling on to the concrete path around the bath. Later, many more were found to have fallen on the grass nearby.

While several theories, from waterspouts to tornadoes, have been proposed to explain such phenomena, none has yet occurred in such a way as to be properly verifiable.

Fortunately my storm is of the more usual sort and the thunder and lightning soon pass – although the rain continues to pelt down. The air smells of ozone, created from oxygen by lightning, and also of petrichor, a chemical released by dry soil after rain. It's exhilarating – though I can't help but hope it eases up a little soon. Sheltering beside the Darent I'm drier than I would be back on the field path, but there's no pretending I'm not getting wet.

William Hazlitt recalls Coleridge, on a trip in Somerset, 'running out bare-headed to enjoy the commotion
of the elements', and while, like him, I enjoy thunder-
storms now, I was horribly afraid of them as a child.
The house opposite ours was struck by lightning one
evening when I was about five, and nothing I have
heard since has ever seemed so loud and so terrifying.
My parents were entertaining friends downstairs: there
will have been vol-au-vents, probably, and Dad's jazz
playing on the record player that Mum had saved up
Green Shield stamps to buy. I had been put to bed in
my Spider-Man pyjamas and wasn't allowed to disturb
them, but the thunderclap ejected me from my bed and
deposited me halfway down the stairs where I sat and
wailed until one of my sisters came to comfort me. But
for many years after that, electrical storms – particularly at night – had a particular, lonely terror.

Eventually, to help me outgrow the memory's power,
I deliberately went outside during a thunderstorm. It was
during my second year at university, and I was shar-
ing a little house in the centre of Oxford with a friend
and my then-boyfriend; he and I climbed out of a tiny
window in the topmost room to sit on the tiled roof as
thunder echoed flatly among the old buildings and lightning struck the towers and spires around. It was only
much later, after we had come in drenched and drunk
on adrenalin and Jack Daniels, that I thought to worry

about the lead guttering we had so cavalierly been resting our feet on.

The trees I'm just as cavalierly sheltering beneath now have their roots in the Darent; but beyond the wide water meadows are hedgerow oaks, and on the heavier clay soil of the ridge, where I stood earlier and admired the view, are sweet chestnuts coppiced on a rough fifteen-year cycle. Before the rain the topsoil there was parched, but most trees draw their water from much deeper down where the earth very rarely dries out, a big tree taking up as much as five hundred litres a day. As moisture escapes from their leaves through transpiration – its rate increased by the hot weather we've been having – it pulls an unbroken column of water up through tubes in the tree's tissue, and the network of roots with their tiny hairs draws in more from the surrounding soil. I remember all this clearly from GCSE biology – I can still picture the diagram of a root in our textbooks, with its neat apical meristem, xylem and phloem vessels – but out there in the fertile Kent countryside, summer rain pelting down, it is as though I can feel it going on all around me: the intake and outbreath of water that's brought the land to life since time immemorial.

Today's rain won't all be taken up by plants and trees, though. A large proportion of it will simply evaporate from the top layers of the soil and the drenched leaves and grass once the sun comes out again; some will find its way by surface run-off or soil interflow into the Darent and away to the Thames; and if enough falls, some will sink down to recharge the chalk aquifer deep below my feet.

The storm relents a little, and putting up the hood of my anorak I set out again. Maize must have been grown somewhere nearby, probably to feed cattle; there's evidence of it in a badger scat by the path. The brocks will be deep in their setts now, snoring in the nests of dry grass or straw that they change regularly; but despite the weather those other burrowers, the rabbits, are seemingly not all underground.

Without the dense under-fur and guard hairs of creatures like hares, rabbits can become wet quite easily – and wet animals lose heat fast. But because they need their food to be over 50 per cent water, rabbits like to feed at dawn and dusk when the dew is down – or when the grass is rain-soaked, as it is now. All I see of this one is a white scut bouncing away into the scrub woodland at the field margin where a dozen more are doubtless waiting for me to pass, eyes wide, ears swivelling, every so often twisting around irritably to groom stray raindrops from their fur.

The meandering course of the Darent straightens as it nears Lullingstone Castle, evidence of past projects to manage its flow and provide power to long-gone mills.

A swan drifts, moored to its dimpling reflection, and a couple of fishermen are sitting out the rain in little tents on the bankside, rods propped above the slow-moving water. According to my map there's a trout lake on the other side of the river, created from old gravel pits, but I'm walking fast now with my head down and don't see it: my lightweight anorak is doing a passable job but my jeans have turned clammy and clinging from mid-thigh down to ankle, and I'm beginning to suspect that my trainers are letting in rain. I leave Lullingstone, and the nearby Roman villa, unvisited.

It's only a mile and a half to Eynsford and its pubs though, and I'd much rather be out in the weather than at work – wet jeans or no. Consulting the damp paper instructions one more time I take a road that tracks the river on its right, with arable fields stretching up and away to the left: some have already seen the combine, but not all. I hope that the sun comes out again and it stays fine for the rest of the harvest; a lot may have changed in modern agriculture, but good weather in late summer is still essential for farmers. A wet grain crop may not be lost any more, but it must be dried before it can be stored, and that costs money.

Eynsford after an August thunderstorm seems a shadow of its usual picture-postcard self: nobody picnicking on the village green, nobody taking photos of the pretty ford and arched bridge. The church crouches stoically, its wet spire aloft like a finger held up to test the weather; the castle looks deserted, and the pub only harbours a couple of punters in polo shirts and deck shoes, a Porsche Cayenne and a BMW Z4 parked out the back. The drenched summer bedding in its window boxes, probably glorious a month ago, looks tired and past its best.

Walking back to the station after a drink and some time spent drying out I search in vain for the remnants of an avenue of trees that my printout tells me were planted as a mnemonic, the first letter of each spelling out a line of a poem by Robert Browning: 'The best is yet to be, the last of life, for which the first was made.' I find an oak for O, a beech, several ashes and a sycamore, but I can't find the variety of species the quotation would surely require – and with the rain still falling, though not nearly as heavily as earlier, I don't linger for too long.

Back at home I check anxiously that the gutter at the front of the house hasn't become blocked and overflowed again; thankfully, it remains clear. Inside I find the dog asleep under my desk, a sure sign there's been thunder here, too. There's a music festival at the weekend that some of my friends are going to and I wonder if the summer storms will clear by then, or whether there'll be Pac-a-Macs and power cuts, cheap tents adrift on flash-flooded fields.

I hope not, of course – yet there's something salutary about the way our best endeavours can still be scotched by something so simple and primordial as the weather: it keeps us in our place somehow, reminds us that we are still part of the natural world, and not above it. Nobody wants rain on their wedding day, and the damage wrought by storms and flooding can be terrible – but imagine a world where the weather had been regulated and tamed, where nothing inconvenient ever happened, and our activities were never curtailed. There'd be no heatwaves nor early frosts; no more wet Wimbledons or mud-fights at Glastonbury. There'd be no lightning storms for Coleridge, or sudden downpours for Swift – and I can't help but think we'd be much the poorer for it.

4

DARTMOOR

October

Mizzle: fine, misty rain

Wind west
Rain's nest.

OLD DEVONSHIRE PROVERB

A few months after she won the Man Booker prize for her novel *The Luminaries*, Eleanor Catton revealed that she had done a lot of hiking as a child, and that her father had given her two pieces of advice about which she had had distinctly mixed feelings. The first was, 'Nature looks more beautiful in the rain,' and the other, 'A view needs to be deserved.'

Both ring true to me – as does her ambivalence. My father's most frequent aphorism when walking with us children on Dartmoor every year was 'Rise above it!': rise above tiredness, frequently, or steep climbs; but very often, rise above rain. The six of us – you may picture us in cheap 1970s cagoules and sodden bellbottoms – grew up loving the moors in all weathers, and it was just as well: as an area of high ground between two sea coasts, Dartmoor does get a lot of orographic, or relief, precipitation, particularly on its western-facing slopes and on the high ground: *'Nine months' winter and three months' bad weather,'* as the local saying goes.

The average October rainfall here is 212 mm – more than double the national average of 94.1 mm. But in the autumn of 1946, 174 mm of rain fell in just twenty-four hours at Princetown, on the high moor. Fortunately the weather isn't nearly as bad as that when we park up at a windswept crossroads not far from the famous Devon village of Widecombe-in-the-Moor. It is raining, though: the kind of thin drizzle, almost mist but quick to soak through clothes, that can blanket the high moor, obscure landmarks and prove treacherous to those who lose their way. 'Dimpsey', the locals call this weather, but while some may find it dull and miserable, as we walk I can almost hear my mother quoting Emily Brontë:

> *The mute bird sitting on the stone,*
> *The dank moss dripping from the wall,*
> *The thorn-trees gaunt, the walks o'ergrown,*
> *I love them – how I love them all!*
> *from* 'A Little While, A Little While', 1838

Born and brought up in Indian hill country, my mother loved the English countryside – Dartmoor particularly – and was capable of a childlike rapture that embarrassed me as a teenager, but which shaped me nonetheless.

Today's walk begins with three tors, then takes us down off the moor through a steep, wooded valley of the River Dart before climbing back up for one final summit and back to the car. The wet weather will make it feel longer than its seven miles, I know, but with four tors to climb it will, at least, be eventful.

We sit in the rain-speckled car to pull on our water-proofs and lace up our boots, the dog whimpering impatiently from the boot. When at last we set out I can almost sense – as though in a timeslip – our later return to the waiting car, sore-footed, tired and triumphant. But there's a long, wet-weather hike to do first.

Joseph Taylor, in his *Complete Weather Guide*, says of October:

> The gloom of the declining year is . . . during this month enlivened by the variety of rich and bright colours, exhibited by the fading leaves of shrubs and trees . . . to these fugitive colours are added the more durable ones of ripened berries, a variety of which now adorn our hedges. The weather during this month is misty, with a perfect calm . . . the fogs during this month are more frequent and thicker than at any other period of the year.

Season of mists, indeed – although the mizzle that chills our faces and hands as we set out and shrouds the distant tors in grey is a distinct step up from that. Taylor is right about the colours, though: the purple heather may have finished flowering but there is still some willowherb and hemp agrimony blooming on the wet roadsides, the hedges are full of sloes and haws and the moors flicker and flame with damp, dying bracken and yellow-flowering gorse.

We cross the empty road and set out for the first tor, a tumble of granite slabs like grey horse dung on the horizon. Underfoot, the rain-soaked moor is a mosaic. Its close, springy turf is starred with tiny yellow tormentil and blanketed in parts with intarsias of purple heather; longer, sandy-coloured moor grass is cropped down in places by cattle. There is also prickly gorse (also known as furze, or whin), which is nibbled into mounds by sheep and often shelters rabbits beneath, and swathes of tall bracken, green in summer and rusting to yellow and brown in autumn – which nothing eats. There are very few trees, though here and there a hawthorn struggles into a bent, wind-wizened shape, and in a couple of places fragments of ancient, stunted oak woods survive among the rocky clitter. These are magical places, as I discovered one day when a sudden rainstorm blew across the moor, driving me to find shelter.

It was my first trip back to Dartmoor since childhood; I was in my mid-twenties, lost and at a low point, and an obscure homing instinct drove me back to the place I had loved as a child. The night before I left London I'd dreamed that the roof space above my tiny bedsit was full of water, the ceiling bulging and dripping onto my bed; a sense of unease dogged me all the way west on the train. I stayed at a shabby B&B in Widecombe whose owners clearly wanted to take care of me, dropping me off in their battered 2CV each day so I could walk the places I remembered. That day I'd set out from Two Bridges and hadn't been walking long when the weather changed; at first, I tried foolishly to shelter under a stile, laughing despite myself as I crouched pointlessly in the lee of its narrow foot-plank, lashed by rain. In a break in the weather I made a dash for Wistman's Wood, where tiny, gnarled oaks footed in moss-covered boulders and hung with beards of lichen and epiphytic ferns protected me from the worst of the downpour that followed. I remember the feeling of being somewhere enchanted, almost out of time; and also the fragile sense of acceptance the half-hour I spent there brought.

Mosses, lichens and bryophytes do well on Dartmoor – as you'd expect from somewhere with excellent air quality and plenty of rainfall. The area became a vital source of sphagnum moss during the First World War when it was gathered in great quantities, dried and sent off to be used in wound dressings due to its absorbency and healing properties; it's been shown to slow the growth of fungi and bacteria. Twelve species are found on Dartmoor, and all can hold eight times their own weight in rain: their slow decay, over thousands of years, is what created the peat that lies over Dartmoor's granite bedrock. Dried sphagnum, prized still for its water-retentive qualities, is available by the sack-load in garden centres for use as a soil conditioner today.

The old man's beard that colonises Dartmoor's pockets of wind-bent trees is also said to have antibiotic and anti-fungal properties. Each unearthly, grey-green, podded cluster slows the rain's progress down from the branches and into the soil, the tangled fronds of lichen dripping long after each shower has passed, slowing evaporation and helping to keep the air in these ancient little rainforests moist.

Usually the views from the high ground are staggering, the moor opening up for ridge after tor-topped ridge all the way to the far-distant sea, but today we can only see for a mile or so. The sky is grey and low, crowding around us like an inverted bowl, and the air is thick and dull. A clear day may make for more pleasant walking and better visibility, but these low clouds and rain are helping to maintain Dartmoor's precious blanket bogs, now seven thousand years old. And anyway, it seems to me that if you only ever go out on sunny days you only see half the picture, and remain somehow untested and callow; whereas discovering that you can withstand all the necessary and ordinary kinds of weather creates a satisfying feeling of equanimity in the face of life's vicissitudes that may or may not be rational, but is real nonetheless. I feel pleasingly resolute as we crouch in the lee of the tor's grey summit to strap a waterproof coat on the dog before setting out for the next tor, a mile or so away across the open moor.

Dartmoor formed from a giant batholith, a slab of once-molten magma that has been weathered down over millennia and had peat accumulate on it to create an upland area of poor, acid soil studded with granite outcrops that mark the densest remaining areas of the impermeable bedrock. Today's rain, light though it is, is part of that weathering process, chemically breaking down the exposed granite and feldspar of the tors and penetrating their fissures until, when winter comes, ice segregation will begin minutely to break the stones apart, eventually producing gravel, quartz sand, silt and china clay. Some of Dartmoor's several hundred tors have become mere scatters of rocky clitter on a hillside, the ghosts of tors long gone; others, like Haytor, still loom vast, monumental and deceptively invulnerable. Most, for now, are somewhere in between.

The sculptor Peter Randall-Page is fascinated by granite and the way it weathers down to produce other rocks like sandstone and shale – not to mention all the soils derived from them. In 1991 he took six Dartmoor moorstones, sculpted them and sited them in the nearby Teign Valley as part of the Common Ground charity's 'Local Distinctiveness' project. One, split in two and intricately carved on its inner faces, sits on a tiny island in the river Teign; another, in a wood, has water flowing from its summit; a third was built into a gap in a dry-stone wall. All are publicly accessible. For him, granite is the most elemental of stones: 'stuff personified' as he calls it, 'quintessentially dumb matter . . . the mother of all rocks'.

We're climbing the second tor's slopes through sodden, browning bracken when we find it: three vertebrae, human-sized, chalk-white but fused between with bright orange cartilage. Next there's a rib, and then another, chewed a little at the ends; then a wide smudge of fleece pounded by perhaps a year's rain into the turf and looking like nothing so much as sodden tissue paper thrown carelessly down. A few paces on we come across a whitened skull with its empty eye sockets and one curly horn; like the vertebrae, it's been picked completely clean by microorganisms, and washed by a winter's worth of rain.

Rain is essential to the process of decay, providing the moisture that fungi and detritivores need to survive. Without enough rainfall, decomposition can slow right down, plant matter desiccating, dead animals – if they are not scavenged – becoming mummified, as saprophytic bacteria and moulds struggle to take hold. Too much rain, though, can be equally bad: prolonged flooding can produce anoxic conditions in the top layers of soil and lead to a rise in toxic by-products of decomposition, such as hydrogen sulphide – which in turn makes it difficult for worms and other invertebrates to survive. Soil fertility depends on the decay of plant and animal matter, aided by five million nematodes, ten million bacteria and ten thousand million protozoa per square metre of soil, and the autumn rain that's falling softly around us today is helping everything rot down, from the browning bells of the heather to horse dung and the remains of this dead sheep.

Not that the living ones we pass seem very bothered. Whiteface Dartmoors, bred to cope with the poor upland grazing (and to withstand the weather), they are 'hefted' or 'leared' to a patch of this unfenced landscape from which they won't stray, and the knowledge of which will be passed down from ewe to lamb: where to take shelter when the rain really sets in, where the best moor-grass is and where water may most easily be found. It won't be long until these ewes are brought down off the moor to be bred, but for now they graze, dirty grey between the grey rocks and sky, utterly unperturbed by the drizzle that beads on their lanolin-rich wool. The Dartmoor ponies with their thick manes and tails are the same, the guard hairs of their winter coats shedding the raindrops easily so their skin beneath remains dry.

After Top Tor the sky lightens slightly and the mizzle fines briefly away, though the sun can't quite break through the low cloud. 'Rain in the air has . . . the odd power of letting one see things in the round, as though stereoscopically,' writes Nan Shepherd in her extraordinary paean to upland landscapes, *The Living Mountain*. 'New depth is given to the vista . . . when the mist turns to rain there may be beauty there too.'

We can see other walkers on the next tor, the bright dots of their wet-weather gear incongruous against the old landscape – as must be our own. Two buzzards wheel easily overhead, looking for carrion or any small mammals that might take advantage of the brief respite from the weather; a fox scat, dissolving in the rain to grey fur and little bones, shows that there are plenty about.

By the time we're coming down off the moor the drizzle has thickened again. We pass through a gate fastened with a lovely old iron latch, twisted and looped and hung with a single silver droplet of rain, and take a little sunken farm track down into the valley. The old bitumen has been entirely lost from the two edges, which now gurgle with fast water; a channel has also been scored through the centre, exposing the loose stones and rubble beneath. It's clear that at some point in the long, wet winter a great quantity of water ran off the moor and down this lane.

Several rivers are born on the moor: the East and West Dart, of course (which meet at Dartmeet), but also the Bovey, Avon, Erme and Plym, the Teign, the East and

West Okement and dozens of tributaries and man-made leats dug to take water to individual farms and hamlets. And on a day like today you can see (and hear) the rain coming down off the moor in a thousand places. Tiny becks and rills, too small even to have a name, creep in creases through peat or make use of paths; water sheets sideways across roads and trickles down field drains; it gurgles at roadsides and swells the moorland streams, where it can find them, until they roar white and unstoppable on stony beds. Thinking about the water coming off the high ground calls to mind Alice Oswald describing the source of the East Dart in her hypnotic, ventriloquial, forty-eight-page narrative poem, *Dart*:

> *I find you in the reeds, a trickle coming out of a*
> *   bank, a foal of a river*
> *one step-width water*
> *of linked stones*
> *trills in the stones*
> *glides in the trills*
> *eels in the glides*
> *in each eel a fingerwidth of sea*
> *   from* 'Dart', 2002

Despite Dartmoor's many blanket bogs and mires, it is considered a 'flashy' catchment area due in part to its impermeable bedrock, which means that when it rains the effects are seen almost immediately in its waterways. When the drizzle falling today on the high ground reaches the sea at Dartmouth it will find a wide, deep-water harbour, very different from the gin-clear, rocky rivers of the high moor with their fast, white eddies and tin-coloured depths. There, at last, it will become part of the sea, only to evaporate, condense, and fall again – perhaps on Devon's uplands – as rain.

The track joins a narrow road between drystone walls and we put the dog on the lead in case of cars. The grazed, improved pasture on each side of the road is so green compared to the upland landscape we've just left. Spiky rushes may be making inroads here and there into damp corners and along the field drains, but these are the green postage stamps of the English imagination, here made from 'newtakes' – no longer newly taken at all – and walled off cleanly from the dull pewter and bronze of the moor above. But cultivation often comes at a cost: not only is unimproved land usually more biodiverse, but it also tends to hold on to water better. A recent study by the Environment and Sustainability Institute, University of Exeter, showed that one square metre of intensively improved grassland held just forty-seven litres of water compared to the 269 litres per square metre held by unimproved 'rhôs' pasture with its naturally occurring purple moor grass and sharp-flowered rush.

The old drystone walls bounding the road where we

walk are shaggy with moss and dog lichen and pinned with medals of pennywort and the delicate buttonholes of maidenhair spleenwort, all beaded silver with rain. A few paces ahead of us a stonechat perches on the top of the wall and flicks his wings insouciantly. The call he makes echoes almost exactly the clash of wet pebbles loosed from the disintegrating road surface under our boots.

We pass through a hamlet where water drips from the eaves of a lovely old thatched longhouse, now with two expensive cars parked outside. A little burn gurgles in a stone-lined channel thick with yellow and brown ash leaves, and a dozen or so fieldfares startle from a garden and cluster into a hedge, a foretaste of the big flocks the coming winter will bring. Then we leave the road and take a semi-sunken path overhung with dripping trees that leads back up onto the moor. It's boulder-strewn, almost like a dried-up river bed, but at one time would have been kept clear for carts and packhorses. The very last of the yarrow and red campion bloom amid the sodden autumn grass and fallen leaves at the edges, and the gate that takes us onto the moor has another lovely, rust-red latch.

I unclip the lead from the dog. She shakes herself, her body turning faster than her waterproof coat can keep up with, and trots on ahead, following narrow, weaving sheep paths that lead up and away from us through the heather.

Here and there are fungi: exploded earthstars filled with damp grey spores, and the fairytale parasols of fly agaric hiding underneath the sodden bracken. Agaric contains both hallucinogens and neurotoxins, helpfully flagged up – unlike some of its duller and more poisonous cousins – by the bright red danger signal of its cap. A wet summer usually means a good autumn for fungi, helping their mycelia to spread and penetrate the ground – although it's thought that several of our native species are now fruiting in spring as well, due to the warmer temperatures brought about by climate change. Some, like the earthstars and puffballs, use rain to trigger the dispersal of their spores, but in common with most fungi that have open, downward-facing gills the fly agaric will wait for a dry day before releasing them to drift where they will on the wind.

At last, there ahead of us is the familiar shape of the final tor on the walk, a place I've felt hefted to all my life, and still am. Easily reached from the road on its other side, it seems recently to have become a favourite with families; when I was growing up, though, there were far fewer tourists on the moor, and when we came here, as we did on every visit, we'd usually have the tor to ourselves.

Its granite bulk is dark with rainwater, but nevertheless we sit for a few moments in the lee of the topmost mass looking out through the smudged, wet air to the valley of the Dart below and the hills beyond. The drizzle patters only very lightly on the hood of my coat, though the bits of my fringe that have escaped it drip in tails. The dog shakes the rain from her ears and waits.

My mother loved this place, and I think about the day when we brought her up here one last time, right at the very end of her life. It was a strange afternoon; it felt to me as though it should have had more shape, more meaning, but none of us quite knew how to give it the significance we needed. Like so many things in life, you just do your best; but for a long time after we all straggled back to our waiting cars, leaving the gritty ash to blow from the tor's top, I thought, every time it rained, of her body passing slowly into the moor around the tor, and becoming part of it, drawn down by the life-giving water and returned slowly to the earth.

EPILOGUE

It was a mild winter, not nearly so wet as the one before. Some snow fell in the north of the country, but there wasn't a great deal anywhere else. Spring arrived unheralded by gales or storms, our landlady got our gutters fixed, and slowly, as the months passed, I stopped worrying each time it rained.

My year of getting wet – and thinking about, and reading about, rain – has broadened and deepened my feeling for the outside world. I'm no longer just a fair-weather walker; I can choose now to overcome the impulse for comfort and convenience that insulates us not only from the bad in life but from much of the good.

I think we need the weather, in all its forms, to feel fully human – which is to say, an animal. It's under our skin: not just psychologically, but physiologically too. New research has revealed that despite our double-glazed homes and brightly lit offices, a tiny but vital part of our brain knows what season it is outside and alters the behaviour of our immune systems accordingly: proof that millennia of evolution in nature – not apart from it – have left their mark.

In any case, to experience the countryside on fair

days and never foul is to understand only half its story. To watch rain pock the surface of a chalk stream, feel mizzle on the chill skin of your face or smell petrichor rising from summer-dry soil is to be baptised into a fuller, older, and more deeply felt relationship with the natural world.

We commonly describe rain as *chucking it down*, *bucketing*, *pelting*, *tipping* and *pouring*, but here in the UK we have a long, rich lexicon of words for wet weather:

All of a pop: an expression describing wet ground (Shropshire)

A **basking**: a drenching in a heavy shower (East Anglia)

Bange: light rain (East Anglia, Hertfordshire)

Beggar's barm: the froth collected by running streams in ditches after rain, or in puddles by the roadside (Northamptonshire)

A **blashy day**: a wet day (Teesdale); bashy (Northamptonshire)

Blatter: a puddle (Yorkshire)

Bleeterie weather: showery weather; also Blirty: changeable and blout: a sudden shower (all Scotland)

Blunk: a sudden squall (England)

Broke up: bad, in terms of the outlook. *'The weather's broke up; we shan't have it fine agen at present'* (Northamptonshire)

Catching or **catchy**: variable, showery, unsettled; of the weather only (Midlands)

Clashy: wet and muddy, as of roads (Yorkshire)

Cow-quaker: a sudden storm in May, after the cows have been turned out to pasture (England)

Dabbly: moist air; adhesive, like wet linen (Suffolk)

A **dag of rain:** a shower (East Anglia)

Dawny: damp (Herefordshire)

Dibble: to rain slowly in drops (Shropshire)

Dimpsey: low cloud producing very fine rain (Devon and Cornwall)

Ding (to rain heavily) and **onding** (a heavy fall of rain) – Doric (north-east Scotland)

Dinge: drizzle; so a dingey day: a drizzly day (East Anglia)

Djew: as a verb, *rain a djew*; as a noun, *djew rain*. Rain or drizzle (Jamaican patois). Also *juu*

Doley: dull (Lincolnshire)

Donk: dripping; poetically and romantically damp (Yorkshire)

Down-come, down-faw: an incidence of rain (Yorkshire)

A **dravely day:** a showery day (Suffolk)

Dreich: dreary, bleak (Scotland)

Dribs: rain which falls in drops from the eaves of thatched buildings (Northamptonshire, Leicestershire)

Dringey: the kind of light rain that still manages to get you soaking wet (Norfolk, Suffolk, Lincolnshire)

Drisk: misty drizzle (Cornwall)

Drounced (with rain): drenched (Suffolk)

Drowking: drooping through lack of rain
(Northamptonshire)

Duke of Spain: Cockney rhyming slang for rain
(London)

Fady, vady: damp, humid weather, often preceding a
thunderclap (Devon, Cornwall, Worcestershire)

Fill-dyke: February, the month of rainfall

Flist: a sudden squall with heavy rain (Scotland)

Fox's wedding: sudden drops of rain from a clear sky
(Gloucestershire, Dorset, Devon). This term is found
all over the world.

Fremd: strange or odd; frequently applied to bad
weather (Teesdale). From the Old English, and related
to Old High German *fremidi*

Gagy: showery (Sussex)

Gally: wet, as applied to land (Herefordshire)

Gosling blast/gosling storm: sudden wind and sleet
(England)

Haar (Cornwall, Scotland, North-East); **harr**
(Lincolnshire): misty rain that drifts in from the sea

Haitch: a slight, passing shower (Sussex, Kent)

Harle: mist or drizzle coming off the sea (North country,
Lincolnshire)

Hash: severe, harsh. Of unforgiving weather (Co.
Durham)

Haster: a violent thunderstorm (England)

Hemple: drizzling rain (West Country)

Henting: raining hard (Cornwall)

Hossing it down: raining hard (Cumbria)

Hoying it doon: raining heavily (North-East)

Hurly-burly: thunder and lightning (England)

Juggin: raining steadily (Lincolnshire)

Kelching: raining hard; worse than *juggin* (Lincolnshire)

Land-lash: high winds and heavy rain (England)

Leasty weather: dull, wet weather (Suffolk)

Letty (Somerset) or **Lattin** (Shropshire): enough rain to make outdoor work difficult. (NB: To let is to disallow, as in 'let and hindrance')

Messengers: small floating clouds separated from larger masses, thought to predict rain. Called *water-dogs* in Norfolk, and *hounds* in Hampshire

Misla: rain; **misla-in**: raining (Shelta; Irish traveller dialect)

Mizzle: small rain (general)

Moky: cloudy, overcast, damp (Yorkshire)

Moor-gallop: wind and rain moving across high ground (Cumbria, Cornwall)

Mungey: moist, damp, close (Northamptonshire)

Parny: rain (Romany language)

Payling: a wind-driven shower. '*The rain payled so agen me, it was quite uncommon*' (Northamptonshire)

Perry (or parrey, parry, pirrie, pirry): a wet squall; half a gale (Lincolnshire)

Pissing down: a vulgar term for raining hard (general)

Planets: extremely localised rain, falling on one field but not another, is said to fall in planets (Northamptonshire)

Plash: a downpour; plashy: wet, watery (Northumberland, Northamptonshire)

Plothering (Leicestershire); **plutherin'** (Lincolnshire): heavy rain

Plype: a heavy sudden shower (the north-east of Scotland)

Posh: a strong shower. '*I dunna want to be ketcht in a posh o' wet!*' (Shropshire)

Raining **forks tiyuns down'ards:** extremely forceful rain (Lincolnshire)

Raining **stair-rods:** precipitation that appears like solid columns of water (England).

Rawkey: damp, misty, and wet underfoot (Cambridgeshire). From Old English *rok*, meaning storm

A **scoor** of rain, similar to a *skite*, though a touch heavier (Scotland)

Scotch mist: the kind of fine rain a Scotsman will barely notice but which will wet an Englishman to the skin (Northamptonshire, Scotland)

Sea fret: a wet mist or haze that comes in from the sea (Yorkshire, Northumberland, the West Country, East Anglia)

Shuckish: unsettled, unpleasant; as of weather, or a journey (Sussex)

Siling down, Siyalin down: heavy rain (Yorkshire, Lancashire, Lincolnshire)

Skew: thick, driving, but short-lived drizzle (Cornwall)

A **skite** of rain: a very quick and light shower (Scotland)

Slappy: wet, rainy, dirty (West Riding of Yorkshire)

Slattery: changeable, with showers (Lincolnshire)

Slobber: thin, cold rain, mixed with snow (Shropshire)

Smirr (Scotland), **Smur** (Suffolk): extremely fine, misty rain

Smither: light rain (East Anglia)

Snivey: raw, cold and sleety (Northamptonshire)

A **sope** of rain: a great deal of rain; similarly a soss (Cheshire)

Spitting: the kind of thin but threatening rain that may at any moment start *stotting*, *plothering* or *siling* down. Spitter: a light shower (Northamptonshire)

Stoach: to churn up waterlogged land, as cattle do in winter; stoachy: muddy, wet (Sussex)

Stotting: raining so hard it bounces up off the ground (Cumbria)

Sunshower: rain that falls while the sun shines (general)

Teem: to rain energetically (Northumberland)

Tetchery weather: cold, wet or uncertain weather (Suffolk)

Thony: damp (of weather) (Northamptonshire)

Thunner-pash: a heavy shower, with thunder (Co. Durham)

Wade: to be intermittent. Applied to sunshine. *'The sun wades, we shall have rain'*

Water-gall: a secondary rainbow said to predict rainy weather (Dorset, Wiltshire, Hampshire). Also *weather-head*

Watery sunshine: a halo around the sun, portending rain (general)

Weet (n): wet weather; weet (v): to rain slightly (Cheshire)

Wetchered: wet through, after being caught out in the rain (Lincolnshire)

Yukken it down: raining hard (Cumbria)

A GLOSSARY OF METEOROLOGICAL
TERMS FOR RAIN

Cloudburst: sudden, intense rainfall of short duration

Convectional rainfall: rain caused by warm earth heating the air above, which rises and condenses at the dew point

Drizzle: fine precipitation with droplets less than 0.5 mm in diameter

Extreme rain: rainfall with precipitation rates exceeding 50 mm per hour

Frontal rainfall: common in the UK due to our latitude, caused by depressions formed when a cold and warm air mass meet

Heavy rain: rainfall with a precipitation rate of between 4 and 16 mm per hour

Light rain: rainfall with a precipitation rate of between 0.25 and 1 mm per hour

Moderate rain: rainfall with a precipitation rate of between 1 and 4 mm per hour

Orographic rainfall: rain caused by air passing over high ground – *see also* Relief rainfall

Rain: precipitation with droplets of 0.5 mm or more

Relief rainfall: *see* orographic rainfall

Serein: rain from a cloudless sky, usually after sunset

Sleet: mixed rain and snow, or snow that partially melts as
   it falls

Very heavy rain: rainfall with a precipitation rate
   between 16 and 50 mm per hour

Very light rain: rainfall with a precipitation rate of less
   than 0.25 mm per hour

Virga: an observable streak or shaft of precipitation that
   falls from a cloud but disappears (sublimates) before
   reaching the ground

ACKNOWLEDGEMENTS

Rain was largely researched and written at Gladstone's Library in Hawarden, Wales, a uniquely inspiring and uniquely welcoming place. I was lucky enough to be writer-in-residence there, and am grateful for the help and support of all its staff including Louisa Yates, Gary Butler, Phil Clement, Siân Morgan and Ceri Williams. I particularly want to thank Peter Francis, the library's Warden, for granting me the residency – and for his ongoing support.

Thank you also to Jenny Hewson and Zoë Waldie at RCW, Katie Bond at the National Trust, Julian Loose, Alex Russell, Kate Ward, Kate Burton and John Grindrod at Faber, and to Paul Binnie for his beautiful illustrations; and to my husband Anthony Young, who, with our rescue dog Scout, steadfastly accompanied me on several rainy expeditions.

Particular thanks must go to Matt Taylor of the BBC / Met Office for his help with meteorological matters, and also to Adrian Colston of the National Trust; to William Davis, Paul Evans, Lewis Heriz, Lucy Ingles, Richard Jones, Al Kitching, Helen Macdonald, Peter Moore, Matt Shardlow, Chris Skinner, Mike Toms and

Richard Wilson, all of whom contributed nuggets of information or steered me away from various rain-based infelicities. Any that remain are entirely my own doing.

Thank you to Alison Brackenbury and Michael Schmidt at Carcanet for permission to quote from Alison's poem 'Brockhampton', published in her 1995 collection '1829'. Thanks also to writer-directors Peter Middleton and James Spinney for permission to quote from their short film *Notes on Blindness: Rainfall*, which features the words of Professor John Hull. The lines from *Dart* by Alice Oswald (2002) are reproduced here with the kind permission of Faber & Faber.

BIBLIOGRAPHY

An Attempt at a Glossary of Some Words used in Cheshire,
communicated to the Society of Antiquaries by Roger
Wilbraham in a letter to Samuel Lysons, printed by T.
Rodd, 1826

Book of Knowledge, attributed to Godfridus, 1758 (various
dates and printings). First published in 1641 as *The
Knowledge of Things Unknowne*

The Cloudspotter's Guide, by Gavin Pretor-Pinney,
Sceptre, 2006

*The Complete Weather Guide: A Collection of Practical
Observations for Prognosticating the Weather*, by Joseph
Taylor, printed by John Harding, 1812

Country Words, by H. G. Ames, Christchurch Publishers,
1998

Defra: Study to assess the welfare of ducks housed
in systems currently used in the UK (Project code
AWO233)

*The Dialect of Craven in the West Riding of the County of
York, with a Copious Glossary, Illustrated by Authorities
from Ancient English and Scottish Writers, and
Exemplified by Two Familiar Dialogues*, Vols. I & II,
by A Native of Craven, W. M. Crofts, 1828

The Fenland, by A. K. Parker and D. Pye, David & Charles, 1876

From Punt to Plough: A History of the Fens, by Rex Sly, Sutton Publishing, 2003

Glossary of Northamptonshire Words and Phrases, with Examples of their Colloquial Use, and Illustrations from Various Authors, to which are added, The Customs of the County, by Anne Elizabeth Baker, Vols. I & II, John Russell Smith, 1854

A Glossary of the Provincialisms in Use in the County of Sussex, by William Durrant Cooper, printed by W. Fleet, 1836

A Glossary of Provincial Words used in Herefordshire and some of the Adjoining Counties, by Sir George Cornewall Lewis, John Murray, 1839

A Glossary of Provincial Words used in Teesdale in the County of Durham, by P. Dinsdale, J. R. Smith, 1849

'Granite': a Cornerstones essay for BBC Radio 3 by Peter Randall-Page, 2014

A Handbook of Weather Folk-Lore, being a collection of proverbial sayings in various languages relating to the weather, with explanatory and illustrative notes, by the Rev. C. Swainson, William Blackwood & Sons, 1873

The History of the Countryside, by Oliver Rackham, J. M. Dent, 1986

The Landscape of the Welsh Marches, by Trevor Rowley, Michael Joseph, 1986

Bibliography

London's Lost Rivers, by Paul Talling, Random House,
    2011

My First Acquaintance with Poets, by William Hazlitt, first
    published in *The Liberal* in 1823

Natural Childhood, by Stephen Moss. National Trust
    report, 2012

*Predicting the Weather: Victorians and the Science of
    Meteorology*, by Katharine Anderson, University of
    Chicago Press, 2005

Prognostication Everlastinge of Ryghte Good Effecte,
    Leonard Digges, London, 1571

Report on national over-abstraction of rivers by the
    National Rivers Authority (Thames Region), 1989;
    cited in River Darent Low Flow Alleviation, 1994
    (NRA)

Under the Weather, by Tom Fort, Arrow Books, 2006

*Unmanned Aerial Vehicles in Environmental Research:
    using UAV data and geostatistical analysis to quantify
    structural differences between unimproved and intensively
    managed grasslands*, by A. Puttock, L. DeBel,
    D. J. Luscombe, K. Anderson and R. E. Brazier,
    Environment and Sustainability Institute, University
    of Exeter, 2014

*The Vocabulary of East Anglia: an Attempt to Record the
    Vulgar Tongue of the Twin Sister Counties, Norfolk
    and Suffolk, as it existed in the last Twenty Years of the
    Eighteenth Century, and Still Exists, with Proof of its*

Antiquity from Etymology and Authority, Vols I & II, by
Robert Forby, J. B. Nichols & Son, 1830
*Weatherwise: the Sunday Telegraph Companion to the
British Weather*, by Philip Eden, Macmillan, 1995